BUFFY

The Dog from Heaven

Gloria Renner

NEWMAN SPRINGS PUBLISHING
320 Broad Street
Red Bank, NJ 07701

First originally published by Newman Springs Publishing 2021

ISBN 978-1-63692-146-4 (Paperback)
ISBN 978-1-63692-147-1 (Digital)

Printed in the United States of America

To my grandsons, Grant and Davin,
who also share my love for animals

Buffy is a little red poodle.
She is so good. Everyone
calls her the *dog from
heaven*.

An angel...

When Dad comes home in
the evening, he calls,
"Where is the little dog
from heaven?"

Our angel.

Buffy, bursting with
excitement, bounces into
his arms, giving him many
wet "kisses."

Like an angel.

At mealtime, she brings her
food dish to be filled.

Like an angel.

When it is bedtime, a tap on the top of her "bed" brings her running, and she goes right to sleep.

Like an angel.

She will fetch her leash
when it is time to go out for
a walk.

Like an angel.

She always walks nicely,
just watching the squirrels,
not tugging to get loose.

Like an angel.

14

Buffy sits in her car seat on family outings.

Like an angel.

One day, Mom went
to the flower garden
and exclaimed,
"Oh no! Why are all the
flowers dug up?"

No one knew because it *couldn't* be the little dog from heaven...

After several days of
having the same spot dug
up, Dad decided to watch
and find out who or what
was doing the digging...

Well, guess what? It *was*
the "dog from heaven"
hiding her chew bones.

Dad found five bones in the
same spot.

24

He patiently explained
to Buffy that bones stay in
the house,

not in the garden.

Buffy then decided, "I guess if I'm going to be the *dog from heaven*, better places to hide my bones would be under the hall rug, behind Dad's chair, or in my bed."

And that's what she did.

Like an angel.

Our angel.

About the Author

Gloria Renner was born in 1928 in Albia, Iowa. She married and raised her children in Illinois before retiring from a fulfilling career in special education. Books and dogs have always been a big part of her life, and the chance to share Buffy's story with children made the opportunity to publish this book special. Gloria now lives on the East Coast, where her home in the woods includes rescue poodle-mix pooches Cameron and Lynwood and kitties Hope and Holly.

CPSIA information can be obtained
at www.ICGtesting.com
Printed in the USA
LVHW072125130921
697749LV00020B/370

9 781636 921464